The
Children'
and
Games Book

The Children's Party and Games Book

Joyce Nicholson

with drawings by
Kris

RIGHT WAY

CONTENTS

INTRODUCTION

The main purpose of this book is to assist parents, teachers, and leaders of children's organizations, when they have to organize a successful party for the entertainment of children, from babyhood up to about twelve.

In this book a large number of ideas is given so that the organizer will be able to select whatever appeals most, and what are the best games or competitions for the kind of party required, and the age that is being entertained.

Parents will also find this book most useful in entertaining their own children with simple games and competitions at home in the evening.

Three Main Aspects

There are three main aspects in planning a party for children, and each one can provide considerable fun for the organizer as well as for the guests.

Firstly, there are the decorations – all the colourful and fancy extras that so delight a child's heart, particularly a small child.

Secondly, there is the entertainment – games, races, competitions and other activities.

Thirdly, there is the catering – an aspect that tends to become more important as the children grow older.

Hard Work Not Necessary

The important thing to remember about all three points is that they need not entail much work. The parent should be able to gain considerable enjoyment from both the preparation and the carrying out of a children's party. Never decide not to give a party because you think it will be too much work. It is not fair to the child. The main thing is to have a party, and it will be a party if the child has two or three friends, a cake with candles, balloons, a few sweets and some savouries and cakes. It need be neither expensive nor tiring.

In the following pages there are numerous games described that need little or no preparation.

Wet Day Changes
If you are caught by a wet day when you have prepared out-of-doors entertainment, you will find a selection of good 'last-minute' games that can be used without any previous preparation.

More Elaborate Parties
On the other hand, if you have the time and energy, it is possible to put extra work and thought into the party and, with a little ingenuity, make it both original and amusing. You will find this will bring you much additional pleasure, both in the work itself and in the reaction of your guests. Anything novel or fancy is appreciated tremendously by children.

'Theme' Parties
One of the best ways to arrange a novel party is to select some theme or motif, and to carry it out through all the different stages of the party – decorations, entertainment, and catering. For example, a 'Nursery Rhyme Party' or a 'Ship Party', or a 'Cowboy Party' are just a few of the theme parties that will be discussed more fully in chapter 13.

Ideas and suggestions are given for all these aspects of children's parties.

The first chapters discuss generally decoration, entertainment and catering. Next there are chapters on first parties and first games, followed by a large number of sections on all different types of games – indoor, outdoor, quiet, noisy, musical, races, etc., etc. Lastly, there is the chapter on novel or 'theme' parties.

If you feel you know all about children's parties in general, as you probably do, and only want a few ideas for games or entertainment, a glance at the index (page 121) will show you quickly where to find many different types of games.

I

INVITATIONS AND DECORATING

The decorating side is more important for children's parties than for those planned for adults. This is particularly so with parties for young children, who eat very little, but love the 'look' of a party. As they grow older, decoration becomes less important, and entertainment and catering more so.

Invitations
Decoration can commence with the invitations. These may be bought or they can be made at home. A wide range of attractive invitations is usually available at any newsagent or card shop. If you decide to make your own, a white sheet of paper with a coloured picture pasted on the top, and the invitation written below, or one folded in two, with the picture on the outside, and the invitation written inside, can be very effective.

Another idea is to cut the invitation out of coloured board to a certain shape, such as a ship or a doll or a dog, with the invitation pasted on to the shape. Alternatively, you can have the shape double, joining in the centre and folding over, with the invitation pasted inside.

Children love these novel invitations, and if you are having a 'theme' party, you will probably find you have to make them, as it is seldom possible to buy cards to fit the theme satisfactorily. This subject is dealt with more fully, and further ideas for invitations given, in the second-last chapter.

The Table
The table should always be made to look as bright, attractive and colourful as possible. It is usual with parties for small

children to give each child a paper hat, paper serviette, and small bag or basket of sweets. A whistle, squeaker or other 'noisemaker' of some sort, or a small present can be added, if desired. If these things are placed at each child's place, the fancy serviette standing up on a mat, the table will look sufficiently bright without any further decoration.

If more is required, streamers can be placed across the tablecloth, or a necklace made of popcorn threaded on cotton can be added to each place. Bottles of coloured soft drink placed down the centre of the table, with streamers tied round their necks, also look colourful.

As the table is invariably the centre of attraction for the small guests, there is no need to decorate the room further. A more festive air can easily be added, however, by a few streamers or coloured paper decorations hung round the walls or on the mantelpiece.

If balloons are to be given to each child, they could be hung round the lights or over the mantelpiece. Do not give the balloons to the guests until they are leaving. They burst very easily, and if you distribute them too soon you will have floods of tears to cope with.

The baskets for the sweets can be either bought or made, or a very simple and colourful effect can be obtained by putting the sweets in a square of coloured Cellophane, and tying this round the top with string or with a rubber band. More details in regard to these can also be found in chapter 12.

The birthday cake will, of course, be decorated according to your own taste, and placed in front of the small host or hostess. The food supplied should also be planned to add to the colour of the table – pink meringues, chocolate iced cakes, jellies, etc.

The birthday table for 'littlies' should look a delight, and it is easy to make it so.

As the children grow older, the extra party frills such as paper hats, balloons, whistles, will be gradually abandoned, but the table should still be made to look most attractive with bright serviettes, coloured jellies, trifles, sweets and cakes.

2

PLANNING THE ENTERTAINMENT

The entertainment one provides at a party will, of course, vary with the age of the children. Chapter 4 is about 'First Parties' for the children who are not old enough for any sort of organized games. Chapter 5 is full of 'First Games' giving some very simple games for children at the age when they are first starting school.

Beyond that the games are not divided into any age group, but are classified according to the type of game. Most of them can be played with equal enjoyment by all ages, only the degree of skill and amount of vigour applied by the participants will vary with the ages. You will be the best judge of what games will be the right age for your particular guests.

There are, however, a few general rules that can be recommended when planning the programme for a party.

1. *Vary the type of games*
Have an energetic type of game followed by a quiet one, and a longer one followed by a short, quick one.

2. *Do not let any game drag on too long*
Seven to ten minutes is long enough for most games. A quarter of an hour should be the outside limit, unless you strike something with which everyone is obviously really enthralled. If that happens, allow the children to go on playing it, even if it means abandoning some of your prepared programme. Before doing this, however, make sure that everyone is enjoying it, not just the vocal few, and don't let it go on until the children have ceased to enjoy it. Always stop a game while children are still enjoying it.

3. *Do not choose games that are too boisterous*

One often hears of party games in which one team of players tries to force the other side from a particular position, or deprive the other side of some particular object. Heaven forbid! All children's parties will become quite boisterous enough, without actually arranging games that involve a 'fight' to start with.

4. *On the whole, avoid those games where only one child has a turn at one time.*

This sort of game keeps all the rest of the party looking on, while one child only is occupied. You will find that those awaiting their turn will either get very bored (if they are polite), or quite out of hand (if they are rowdy). It is much better to have games where all can join in at once. This does not apply to races, which are always good fun. In these, five or six can take part in each heat, and the onlookers will enjoy cheering on the winner. Nor does this apply to a small party where the children will not have to wait so long, nor to such things as a 'lucky dip' where children will gladly wait to get a present.

5. *Have your list of games written out*

It is amazing how easy it is to forget something in the rush, and perhaps completely overlook a prepared game. Although children's parties need not be hard work, they undoubtedly need more concentrated attention than most forms of entertainment, so have your programme written out beforehand to avoid overlooking anything.

6. *Have everything ready for every game*

If there is any delay at all between games, you will once again find the polite children getting bored or fidgety, and the rowdy ones fighting or damaging your furniture. Make sure, therefore, that you have everything ready beforehand, in order, in some place that is easily accessible to you, but not in sight of the children.

7. *Have a large number of small prizes*

In races or games where a winner is declared, a prize of some sort will usually be expected. It is much better to have a large number of inexpensive gifts for prizes, rather than two or three large costly ones. It is then possible to give several prizes for every competition, so that many share in them. Give prizes for first, second and even third in heats of races, as well as for the finals, and give small prizes to the five or six best in other games.

3

WHAT TO EAT ?

This, of course, is not a recipe book, but some general ideas as to menus can be given.

First Parties

Up till about five or six years old, children eat very little at parties. They are usually slow eaters, anyway, and are often too excited to do more than nibble. The sight of the table seems to overwhelm them, and they tend just to sit and stare. At a party for this age, you will frequently see little ones do no more than eat a few sweets, some ice-cream and drink orange squash.

Also, at this early age, it is most undesirable to provide a lot of rich food. The look of the table, the coloured hats, balloons, etc., are of greater importance than the food. Parents will not thank you if you put too many sweets in front of their children.

Sandwiches and bread and butter and nonpareils ('hundreds and thousands'), are always popular. In addition to these, just a few biscuits and cakes are all that is necessary. If the biscuits are made in the shape of animals, and the cakes made colourful by their icing and decoration, this adds quite enough party atmosphere without the food being rich.

A small helping of ice-cream and/or jelly can be given at the end. A piece of the birthday cake, wrapped in a serviette, is usually given to each small guest as he or she leaves.

Appetites Grow

As they pass this early stage, appetites will, of course, grow larger. Cocktail sausages and sausage rolls become very popular, and are eaten in large quantities. Many children seem to prefer attractive savoury things to too many sweet things.

Time of Party

Once the early party stage is passed, the catering will be affected by what time the party is held, and this time will, of course, vary as the children grow older, and according to bed-time customs.

It is difficult to say at exactly what age the afternoon parties should give way to tea-parties and then to evening parties. It is something you will need to decide for yourself, and it will depend on what sort of party you wish to give, and what the other families in your circle are doing. Also, by this time, your children will begin to have strong views on the matter themselves, and they will probably tell you what sort of party they want, and what time it is to be.

Possibly anything from eight to ten years of age would see the end of the afternoon tea parties, unless an afternoon visit to a film or a pantomime was proposed by way of entertainment. That would be suitable for any age.

Dinner Parties

Once you leave the afternoon tea parties, you may prefer to go straight to evening parties, leaving out the dinner or tea party stage, which is undoubtedly more work. However, it is a good way to entertain the between-age group, as it lets them get home and to bed reasonably early.

It involves asking the children to come at about four or five o'clock, often straight from school, playing some games, then having tea or dinner, playing more games, and finishing at about nine o'clock. A fairly substantial meal needs to be supplied for this sort of party, as the children, particularly if they come straight from school, are usually hungry at this hour. Some people prefer to dish up a proper dinner of soup, meat-course and sweets, rather than bother with all the bits and pieces of fancy party fare. The alternative to this is sandwiches, sausage rolls, savouries, cakes, sweets, etc. You can decide yourself which you would rather do, as both are suitable.

Evening Parties

The evening parties are the last development, and are probably the easiest for the hostess. Guests are asked for about seven or eight o'clock, according to their ages, games are played and supper served at about nine or ten o'clock.

Remember this Point

Whatever time-span you select for your party, make it quite clear in your invitation, whether it is written or verbal. State clearly what time you want your guests to come and what time the party is to end. Parents of guests prefer to know at what time you wish them to call for their family, and, from your point of view, at the end of a strenuous children's party, there is nothing worse than having a tired child or two for an extra hour, owing to some misunderstanding over times.

4

FIRST PARTIES

Children's first parties are, in some ways, the most difficult. One has to cater for both mothers and children and there is little one can do in the way of organized games to entertain the children. It is, however, a very pleasant way to see one's friends and their children. Later on, you only see a crowd of children, a number of whom you do not know, and most of whom take very little notice of you.

It is not much use trying to organize games for children until they are about four years of age. It takes a trained person to do it, and most little children prefer to play round on their own with various toys, or stay with their mothers.

The following are some general suggestions as to what can be provided for the children. Many may seem very obvious, and will certainly be well known to any mother who ¦has attended many children's parties. To the inexperienced ones, however, who are facing the prospect of giving their first children's party, some advice may be helpful.

Toys
A good supply of tricycles, scooters, prams, toys, etc., should be ready on the lawns or inside. If one's own supply is not sufficient, these can be borrowed from friends and relatives. A swing is always popular.

Slide and Merry-Go-Round
If something more elaborate is required, a slide or small wooden merry-go-round that is pushed by hand, can be hired in some places. These are always greatly appreciated, and a slide, particularly, is invariably a success. Small

children will happily queue up and slide down for the whole afternoon.

Moving Pictures

For families able to own, borrow or hire a video, there is no better way of entertaining small childen than by pictures. Suitable films or shows can be hired very easily and children will love them. It keeps them quiet and clean as well as thoroughly happy for the afternoon, and does not exhaust the parents. Small children prefer those films in which real animals appear or real live children take part, rather than animated cartoons, although all are popular.

Scissors, Paste, Pencils and Paper

One other very successful way of amusing three- and four-year-olds, but which involves some organization, is to set them to work with paper, scissors, coloured pencils and/or paste. It may involve borrowing small tables and chairs from your local play group to achieve the happiest results, though the children can be put to work on the floor.

They will be very happily entertained if you give each child a pair of blunt-ended scissors and an old magazine for cutting out coloured pictures.

Tear out all the suitable pages from the magazines – the women's ones are the best – and give three or four to each child, plus a pair of blunt-ended scissors. If you care to carry it further and let the children paste the cut-out pictures on to sheets of paper, it will add even more to their enjoyment.

Alternatively you can give them white or brown paper with coloured pencils for colouring and then scissors to cut out what they colour, or, again, they love cutting out shapes from sheets of coloured paper and pasting these shapes on to sheets of white or brown paper.

There would have to be constant supervision for this sort of play, of course, and it could not be done on good carpets or tables, but it can be guaranteed to entertain.

Plasticine

Four-year-olds can also be entertained with a stick of plasticine each, as suggested on page 22.

Bubble-Blowing
Bubble-blowing, also described on page 28 is another form
of entertainment that would fascinate four-year-olds. Think
twice about it, however, and only have it on a very hot day.
Remember party-frocks and the mess that young children
can get themselves into with a very little bit of water.

If some sort of games are particularly required, the following are very simple and can be enjoyed by three- and four-
year-olds.

Peanut Hunt
Hide a number of peanuts or paper covered sweets in the
garden or inside in very obvious places, and set the children
looking for them. Let them keep what they find, and give a
small prize for the one who finds the most. Keep a few in
reserve to give to the ones who manage to find only a few or
none at all – there are sure to be some.

Pinning the Tail on the Donkey
Pin a large drawing of a donkey or a pig, without a tail, on a
wall or back of a door, marking clearly where the tail should
go. Have a tail made separately. Then blindfold each child,
and, starting him from a mark, a few feet from the donkey,
give him the tail and let him try to place it as near as possible
to where it should go. It is as well not to have an actual pin
for very little children. Pin it where they place it, or mark
each child's attempt, and give a prize to the one who gets it
nearest to the correct position.

Lucky Dip or Fishing Pool
Small children love a lucky dip. Buy a number of small, very
inexpensive presents, enough for at least one, or possibly
two, for each guest. Stores usually have a good selection of
these for a small cost. You can buy several of the same
article. It is a good idea to buy presents that all children will
like. Do not differentiate between girls and boys.

Wrap them in brightly coloured paper. Place them in a
container of some sort – a bucket, wastepaper basket or

clothes basket. Then let each child pick a parcel in turn.

If you can fill the container with sawdust or shavings so that the children have to feel for the present, it adds to the fun (and the mess!). But it is not at all necessary. The children rather like seeing the shape of the parcels and trying to decide which to choose. I certainly would not recommend shavings or sawdust, if it is to be held inside.

An alternative to the Lucky Dip is a 'Fishing Pond'. Erect a screen of some sort with the words 'Fishing Pond' written on cardboard on the outside. Have someone hidden behind the screen with the parcels. Have a fishing line – either a proper one or one made from a piece of smooth stick with string attached and a hook or safety pin tied on the end.

Allow each child to cast the line over the screen in turn, whereupon the person behind attaches a present, which is then pulled over by the child. This will delight small children.

The Mothers

At these first parties it is, of course, necessary to have afternoon tea for the mothers. There is some difference of opinion as to the best time to serve this.

Some have the children's party first, and then send the children out to play, and give the adults their tea. This tends to make the mothers' tea too late, and is sure to be interrupted continually by children coming in and out of the room.

The second plan is to serve the adults first, but this is rather unfair on the children. If they realize it is going on, they are sure to come in, and want something to eat, so the parents' pleasure will be spoilt.

Probably the best idea, if it can be managed, is to serve everyone together. Have the children's party table in the centre of the room, with a small table at one end with the adults' tea set out on it. In this way the mothers can stand round, have a cup of tea and something to eat, while still keeping an eye on their children. They will not be continually interrupted all the time, will enjoy their tea, and they will know what the children are doing.

5

THE FIRST GAMES

In this chapter are some of the simplest games that children of five or six years will love to play. This is the age at which they will be starting school, and will be accustomed to being organized.

It may also be the age at which girls may want to ask all girls, and boys all boys to their parties, probably mostly their school friends.

You will also find games very suitable for five- and six-year-olds in the chapters 8 and 11 on MUSICAL GAMES and RACES, both of which are tremendously popular with young children.

AT THE ZOO

Have all the children sitting on the floor in front of you, and arm yourself with a bag of sweets. Tell them you are a Zookeeper, and that you will describe some of your animals to them. As soon as anyone recognizes the one you are describing, that child puts up his or her hand. If the answer is correct, throw the child a sweet.

MODELLING

Give each child a stick of plasticine, two used matches and a white card, and ask him or her to make whatever animal or figure he chooses. The completed work of art should be mounted on the card, on which the modeller's name is written by an adult, and all displayed as in a picture gallery. Younger children will have a lot of fun with this.

ROB THE SHOP

This is a team race particularly suitable for younger children, so it is included here instead of in the chapter on races. Divide the children into teams, and place them at an equal distance from a circle at the end of the room or lawn. In the circle, have a collection of small but attractive objects, one for each player. They could either all be sweets of some sort, in which case the circle would be called 'The Sweet Shop' or small toys, thus naming the circle 'The Toy Shop'.

At the word 'Go', one member of each team runs up, picks up an object from the circle, then runs back to his place, followed by the second member of the team, who does the same thing. The first team to have all its members home, wins. Players are allowed to keep the object they collect. Children will love this novel race.

TOM TIDDLER'S GROUND

This is similar to the previous game, but is played individually, with prizes going to the quickest only. Have one part of the garden or lawn marked off as 'Tom Tiddler's Ground', and have this area scattered with sweets or toys. One guest is elected as 'Tom Tiddler', and has to guard the 'treasure'. All the other boys or girls stand outside the area, and try to run in and grab one of the sweets, peanuts or toys. If they are tagged (touched) by Tom Tiddler before they get outside the area, they have to give up their booty and drop out of the game. The game finishes when all players are tagged, or all the treasure gone. Only have small things for this game, as some children will get a lot and others nothing.

LUCKY DIP OR FISHING POND

Another way to give all your guests a small gift is to have a Lucky Dip or 'Fishing Pond', as described on page 19, chapter 4. This is a form of entertainment that will be just as thoroughly enjoyed by the five- and six-year-olds as younger children.

PAPER DOILY

Give each child a sheet of paper and a pair of scissors, and ask them to make a paper doily. Have an example to illustrate how this is done. The sheet of paper is folded over several times, until only a few inches square. Small circles, squares or diamonds are then cut out separately round the four sides of the small square. When the sheet is opened out a very pretty pattern results. Give a prize to the most attractive or most original. Children enjoy making these patterns.

PAPER DOILY

WHAT AM I LIKE?

Divide the players into two lines. On one side give all players the name of an animal, on the other the name of a flower. Taking it in turns, a player from one line steps up to a player in the other line, and asks 'Do I look like a daffodil?' (naming his flower). The other player answers: 'No, you look like a hippopotamus' (naming his animal). This question and answer must be requested three times, without the two concerned smiling or laughing. Others may laugh as much as they like. If anyone whose turn it is smiles at all, he or she must drop out. The last one left in is the winner.

FIND YOUR PAIR

Form the children into two circles, one inside the other, with the players of one circle facing the players of the other. Ask them to join hands with their opposite player in the other circle. These two become a 'pair'. They then drop their hands and the two circles either march or run round in opposite directions. At a given signal all players run to join hands with their 'pair' and then flop down on the ground. The last pair down is out each round.

THE GREAT GREY-GREEN GREASY LIMPOPO

The Limpopo river is marked out in the centre of the room or (preferably) lawn, by lines going right across from one side to the other about ten feet apart. One player is chosen to be the crocodile.

The other players try to run back and forth across the river without being caught. If the crocodile tags them, they join the crocodile in the river and help catch the others running back and forth. The last one caught wins. One end of the crocodile must always stay in the river.

PLAYING TRAINS

Form players into pairs with one player left over. Each pair forms a train, with the front one the engine and the second one a carriage clasping the engine round the waist. The

trains then set off chuff-chuffing round the lawn. The odd
player tries to grab on to the back of one of the trains. If
successful the engine of that train has to drop off and grab
on to the back of another train. Lots of noise and fun.

SHOE SCRAMBLE

Ask all the children to take off their shoes, and mix them up
in a big heap in the centre of the room (or the lawn, if the
grass is dry). Then stand the children in a ring round the
heap of shoes. At the word 'Go', all players run to the heap,
and see who can find their shoes and put them on the
quickest.

Give a small prize to the first half dozen properly shod.

TOMMY TUCKER

Form the children into a circle, with one in the centre. This one walks round the circle, and then suddenly stops before two players. He puts his right hand out between them, and then says: 'Tommy Tucker, run for your supper.' On the word 'supper', but not before, the two marked players run round the outside of the circle in opposite directions. The one first back to the vacant space, becomes the next Tommy Tucker, and goes into the centre of the ring. If you like you can make it that the players have to skip, walk or hop instead of run.

TOMMY TUCKER

BUBBLE BLOWING

This may or may not appeal to you. It has its obvious drawbacks, and should certainly only be played on a very hot day with a small party. You can be certain the children will enjoy it. Have a large, shallow bowl of soapy water in the centre of the lawn. Add a little glycerine to the water to give the bubbles a prismatic effect. Supply each child with an ordinary drinking straw or a bubble ring and have a bubble-blowing competition. Let them all blow together, of course, and they will have tremendous fun. See who can blow the biggest bubble, the one that lasts the longest, or goes highest in the air, or who can get the most bubbles from one blow.

CAT AND MOUSE

CAT AND MOUSE

Players stand in a circle, holding hands. One child stands inside the circle and is called the mouse. Another stands outside the circle and is the cat. The cat tries to catch the mouse, but players hinder the cat by raising or lowering their arms and not allowing the cat to break through the circle. You can have two or three cats and mice at a time. This makes it harder to keep the cats out of the circle.

When the cat or cats catch the mouse or mice they join the circle and other children have a turn.

WHAT'S THE TIME MR. WOLF?

One player, Mr. Wolf, stands at one end of the room or lawn, while the rest, who are rabbits, stand at the other end, behind a line. The rabbits all call out: 'What's the time, Mr. Wolf?,' to which Mr. Wolf replies, 'One o'clock,' or 'Five o'clock,' or any number up to 12. According to what is called the rabbits take so many hops forward. This is done several times, until the rabbits are quite near Mr. Wolf. Then, when Mr. Wolf thinks the time auspicious the sudden answer to the oft-repeated question will be 'DINNER TIME'. At this call, the rabbits all turn and run for the safety of their line. Anyone caught by Mr. Wolf before reaching the line, then has to become a wolf, and join Mr. Wolf at the front.

The procedure is repeated, and this time, although the original Mr. Wolf does the answering, there will be others to help catch the dinner at the call of 'DINNER TIME'. As the game progresses, the number of wolves will increase, and the rabbits will become fewer and fewer. The winner, of course, is the last rabbit left alive.

BLIND MAN'S BUFF

This old and popular game can be played in many ways, and young children always enjoy it. The simplest form is to blindfold one child, who will try and catch one of the others, who dance round. If successful, the 'blind man' tries to guess the one caught, and if correct, they change places. If wrong, someone else has to be caught. Never let one child go on being the blind man too long.

HOKEY-POKEY

This is a variation of 'Blind Man's Buff' and a much better game, as it gives the blindfolded child a better chance. Form the players into a circle with the blindfolded one in the centre, with a rolled-up newspaper to hold. Turn this player three times. He then finds his way over to some member of the circle and taps him with the newspaper saying 'Hokey-Pokey?' This player replies by saying 'Hokey-Pokey' three times, and the blindfolded player tries to guess who it is. If correct, they change places. If not, try again! Once again, do not let a player have more than three or four attempts.

This game can be varied by altering the wording of the question and answer, or by having the circle of players walk round the one in the centre, who will stop them by some signal and then point to one of them.

HOKEY POKEY

PUSSY WANTS A HOME

This is another game with many variations. One form goes
as follows. The children all sit or stand in a circle with one
in the centre. This player has to go round the circle saying:
'Pussy wants a home, please.' While doing this, any two
players in the circle can signal to each other and change
places, and Pussy runs to try and get one of their places. The
daring players will have a lot of fun with this, but it can be
difficult for Pussy to get a home. If not successful, 'Mice,
Mice' can be called, whereupon everyone has to change
seats and then Pussy should manage to grab one.

A better variation is to number all members of the circle.
The one in the centre calls two numbers. These two have to

change places. This makes it easier for the centre player to get a place, as the two called may be on opposite sides of the circle, and they are forced to change. If left to themselves, they would not try.

This can be further varied by calling the game 'Fruit Basket', and giving all players the name of a fruit; or 'Animal Corner', and giving everyone the name of an animal, or 'King Neptune', and giving everyone the name of a fish. In each case the one in the centre calls two of the names and those two have to change seats, the centre person trying to grab one of the empty seats.

FOX AND GEESE

Form all players except one into a line, each one clasping the waist of the one in front. These are the geese. The one who is kept out becomes the fox. The fox tries to catch the last goose in the file, which the file tries to prevent by twisting and twirling about. The first one in the file, the leader, who is the only one with arms free, tries particularly hard to protect the flock, by flapping arms like wings and pushing the fox away. When the fox finally catches the end goose (it is no good trying for a middle one), the fox then grabs on to the end of the file as last goose, and the leader becomes the fox. The player behind the leader becomes the leader. In this way, each will have a turn as fox and leader.

TWOS AND THREES

Players form into groups of three. Two of each group hold both hands so as to enclose the third one between them.

FOX AND GEESE

Two players who are left over have to chase one another.
The one who is being chased can be saved by ducking into
the circle made by one of the groups of three. The one in the
centre of that group then has to hop out and become the
chased player. This player can take refuge in the same way
in one of the other 'threes'. Frequent changes make a lot of
fun, and when someone is finally caught, that child will
become the chaser.

*A number of very well-known games, such as 'Oranges and
Lemons', 'Gathering Nuts in May', and 'Drop the Handkerchief' have not been included in this book, firstly, because we
think you will know about them, and, secondly, because we
think your party will be more successful if you entertain the
children with games that are not so well known.*

6

ENERGETIC GAMES

The games in this chapter are all fairly energetic, lots of fun, and need some preparation beforehand to have the right 'props' ready. Never keep children waiting while you go to find what is needed for the next game. Have everything ready in the right order before the party.

CHOCOLATE RACE

This is a game we can guarantee will be a hilarious success with boys and girls. A 100gm or 200gm block of chocolate on a plate, with small knife and fork, is placed on a bridge table in the centre of the room. The best chocolate is that with the small squares.

The guests sit on the floor in a circle round the table, not too near to it, and take turns in throwing a dice. Each player has one throw, then passes it to the next player. If a six is thrown, that player, after passing the dice on, jumps up, runs to the table and cuts off one square of the chocolate and eats it, without touching it with fingers. After swallowing the first piece, the player then cuts another piece and as many as possible, one at a time, until some other player throws a six, who will then take his or her turn at the table, the first player returning to his or her place.

The excitement is intense, and some players, after throwing a six, will barely reach the table before another player rushes up. As soon as the new player comes up, of course,

CHOCOLATE RACE

the player there has to put down the knife and fork, possibly without even a taste, while others may have time to cut and eat five or six squares of chocolate!

OLD CLOTHES SHOP

You may or may not like the sound of this suggestion. Ask all the guests to bring a set of old clothing – hat, shoes, dress or suit, coat, gloves, etc. – which are to go to a needy charity. When they have all arrived, stand the guests in a circle, each holding his bundle of clothes. Start some music and tell players to start passing their bundles round the circle to their right. When the music stops, all guests have to put on the clothes they find themselves holding and stay in them for the rest of the party. Alternatively, you can ask guests to dress up in the clothes they bring.

This dressing up will cause a great deal of amusement, but you would have to be sure your guests were the right sort before trying it. They could just stay in the old clothes for half an hour or so.

POSTING LETTERS

This is an unusual game that appeals to younger children enormously but needs rather elaborate preparation. The children would need to be old enough to read. Hide around the garden or house about half a dozen letter boxes. Do not make them too difficult to find. They would be easiest made from the old cardboard cartons that are readily available from the supermarket, or they could be made from shoe

boxes. Paste them shut top and bottom, or paste the lids on, then make a posting slot in one side, and paint them a bright colour. Mark each one with the name of a town or country, or, with younger children, you could choose designations such as 'The Zoo', 'School', 'The Circus', 'The Sweet Shop', 'The Aquarium', 'The Beach'.

Give each child half a dozen envelopes, with the posting places marked on them. Also write the child's name on the back of each of his envelopes. The one who finds the six letter-boxes posts his letters, and returns to the organizer first, is the winner. When the game is completed, open the letter-boxes and check all the envelopes inside (warn them that this will be done). You will then be able to make quite sure that the winning children have posted their letters in the correct boxes, as their names will be on the backs of the envelopes.

HIT THE FOOTBALL

Divide the players into two teams, and stand each behind a line at different ends of the lawn. Place a light plastic football in the centre, and supply each player in each team with a tennis ball. At the word 'Go', the players in each team throw their tennis balls at the football, trying to drive it over the line at the opposite end. Members of one team can, of course, collect any of the tennis balls from the opposing team that come down their end, and throw them back at the football, but they must not over-step their lines. The game ends when the football is driven over one of the lines, or when all tennis balls are out of reach. In that case the team will win which has driven the football nearest the opposing line.

This is strictly an outside game, for rather older children, and one to be watched closely, as you don't want the children throwing the balls at each other rather than the football.

CIRCLE BALL

Stand all guests in a circle, with one player in the centre. Those in the circle throw a tennis or basket-ball to each other, either around or across the circle. The player in the centre tries to catch it. If successful, the one who threw the ball takes his or her place. If anyone drops the ball, the one

dropping it must pick it up, and if the centre player gets it first, the one who dropped the ball must take the centre position.

Once again, a strictly outside game for children who are old enough to throw and catch, and one you should not let get too boisterous.

STOP THE BALL

Form the players into a circle, each player standing with feet apart, touching the feet of the person on either side. One player stands in the centre with a beach or basket-ball. He tries to roll the ball out of the circle between the legs of the children forming the circle. They, in turn, try to stop the ball with their hands (they must not move their feet), and roll it back. If the ball breaks through, the player through whose legs it goes takes the centre position.

FEEDING-TIME

Divide the children into teams of four or five, who each select a leader, and give each team the name of some farm animal – horse, pig, cow, hen, rooster, dog, cat, etc. Scatter around the garden or inside the house a large number of sweets, peanuts or other objects. At the word 'Go', everyone is to start looking for these sweets, but only the leader of each team can pick them up. When any team-member finds a treasure, he or she stands over it and makes the animal noise of the team. The hens cackle, the pigs grunt, etc. The leader, on hearing one of the group calling, rushes to the place and collects the booty. Once a player has found a treasure and is standing over it, making a call and protecting it, it cannot be collected by the leader of another group. There must be no fights about this. The leaders, of course, have a busy time, rushing from place to place, answering the calls of their team members, and the team whose leader collects the most objects wins.

SPINNING THE PLATTER

All players sit in a circle, and are numbered, beginning with 'one'. One player stands in the centre and is given a tin plate. He or she spins this round and calls a number. The

person whose number is called has to hurry and grab the plate before it stops spinning. If successful he or she returns to position. If unsuccessful, this player becomes the centre player.

BLOW CIRCLE

Divide the guests into groups, each group to form a circle by joining hands. Then give each group a feather or a balloon

and see which one can keep the feather or balloon in the air the longest by blowing it. Players must not let go of each other's hands.

✿ BLOW TENNIS ✿

This is similar to the above game, but played with two teams only. Tie a string about shoulder high across the room, or between two posts or trees outside. The teams stand one on each side of the string and a balloon or a feather is put into play. The teams have to blow this back and forth over the string. The team that lets it fall to the ground on their side, or blows it under the string, loses. Players may not touch the balloon with their hands. There will be a lot of fun caused by this game, and if players start to laugh, of course, it is very hard for them to keep blowing.

BLOW PING-PONG

This is another hilarious game, similar to the two above, this time played round a table. It is only suitable for a small party. Have two teams, members of which kneel on either side of the table. A ping-pong or table-tennis ball is placed in the centre of the table, and each team tries to blow it off the table on the opposite side, at the same time blowing

strenuously to prevent the opposition team first blowing it over their own side. Hands must be kept off the table. If anyone touches the ball with any part of the body – hands, head or shoulders, the team the other side of the table gains a point, and you can set a winning score of five or ten points to end the game – or when everyone is exhausted.

7

QUIET GAMES

The following games are quiet games, though extremely interesting, and require a certain amount of thinking and concentration from guests. They also require some preparation on the part of the hostess.

HAT PARADE

Give each player two or three sheets of newspaper and a good supply of pins. Supply several pairs of scissors, though not necessarily a pair each. All players have to make a hat, and then wear it. The prize, of course, goes to the one voted the best.

DENTISTS AT WORK

Supply each guest with some red Plasticine and a handful of peanuts, and ask them to make a set of false teeth. The result will cause plenty of laughter.

DENTISTS AT WORK

MAKE AN ELEPHANT

An evening game that always causes laughter. Give each guest a sheet of newspaper. Then turn out the lights, and ask them to 'tear out' an elephant from the sheet. When the lights go on again, see who has achieved the result.

This is an excellent game for adapting to any particular party, where you want a theme repeated throughout. Players can be asked to tear out anything that suits your theme – a doll, a merry-go-round, a cricketer, a cowboy, a Christmas tree, etc.

Also, it need not be played at night. Even in daylight, it is quite hard to tear out a good shape.

PROFESSION PLAY

Divide your guests into pairs. Each pair then draws a slip of paper from a hat or box, prepared before the party. On each slip is written a profession or trade of some sort – Doctor, dentist, dressmaker, nurse, shop assistant, teacher, bricklayer, plumber, carpenter, lawyer, judge, policeman, etc., etc. Each pair in turn then has to act their profession, while the rest of the guests guess what it is. A lot of fun will be caused by some of the actions.

GUESS HOW MANY

This is an unusual game, which will attract and keep the attention of boys and girls of most ages. Have a number of saucers placed at equal intervals around a table. The saucers will be numbered from 1 upwards, and on each saucer will be a small pile of some particular objects. For example, on one saucer will be a small pile of matches, on others a pile of peas, a pile of shelled peanuts, melon seeds, beads, screws, nails, a pile of popcorn, hundreds and thousands (not too many of these, as you have to count them!), barley, pennies, rice, a piece of paper with a lot of pencil dots on it, etc., etc. You, of course, will have counted and noted beforehand how many of each article is on each saucer.

Give each player a pencil and paper, and ask them to go round guessing how many objects are on each saucer. Get them to write down the numbers of the saucers on the left-hand side of their sheets of paper, one below the other, before they start, and then, as they move around the table, they can put opposite each number how many of the particular objects displayed they think are on that saucer.

GUESS HOW MANY

You will need to work out beforehand some system of allotting points for the final results. For example, anyone getting the exact number for one saucer, gets 10 points; within 5 of the correct number, 5 points; within 10, 3 points; within 12, 2 points; within 15, 1 point. This will depend on how many of each object you put on the saucers.

FAMILY ALBUM

The family album is often looked upon as rather a joke these days, but it can become the basis for a very amusing and absorbing game for older boys and girls. Divide your guests into four, five or six groups (about five or six to a group), and give each group an album you have prepared beforehand. Make this from about six sheets of brown paper or foolscap, folded across the centre, and either stitched together or fastened with paper fasteners. Label each one 'Family Album' on the front.

Then have each group select one of their members whose family album it is to be, and get them to write the following headings across the tops of the pages, leaving two pages where more than one picture is called for: 1. Childhood Scenes; 2. Pictures of School-days; 3. First Sweetheart; 4. Wife or Husband; 5. Relations; 6. Children; 7. Home; 8. Hobbies; 9. Work; 10. What the Future Holds.

Then provide each group with a number of old magazines, scissors, and paste, and get them to cut out and paste in suitable pictures on each page. Some of the results will be very amusing.

ADVERTISEMENTS

This game can be played in two ways. Collect a number of well-known advertising slogans from newspapers, magazines, leaving out in each case the actual name that is being advertised. Make a list of these, numbered from 1 upwards, and have copies typed out, with a space left opposite each slogan for the product it is advertising to be written in. Give each guest a list and a pencil and see how many of the slogans they recognize.

Alternatively, cut out from magazines and newspapers a number of well-known advertisements, again deleting in each case the actual name; paste them on sheets of paper, number them, and pin them up round the walls. Give competitors pencil and paper and get them to walk round seeing how many they can recognize, the names of which they will write down opposite the relevant numbers on their sheets of paper. This second method is more trouble, but undoubtedly makes a more interesting game.

MEMORY TEST

Give all guests pencil and paper. Bring in a tray with about 20 to 25 small articles on it, all clearly visible. Have a good variety of things, such as a fountain pen, an orange, a peg, a cup, a spectacle case, a paint-brush, pair of scissors, etc. Leave the tray in the centre of the room for a few minutes and then take it away. Players have to write down as many of the articles as they can remember. The winner is the one with the most correct. Take off two points for any articles written down that were not on the tray.

YES-NO BEANS (WITH A DIFFERENCE)

The usual way to play this game is to give each player a number of beans, peas, or beads – about ten. Guests then have to move round the room, talking to each other. If one player can get another one to say 'Yes' or 'No' during the conversation the successful player hands over a bean. The idea, of course, is to get rid of all your beans. The player doing so first, is the winner.

Playing it in reverse may appeal more. Give each player about 5 to 10 sweets or peanuts. Any player who can get another player to say 'Yes' or 'No' in answer to a question, *collects* a sweet or peanut from that player. The one who has the most sweets at the end of a certain time is then the winner, and already has the reward.

MEMORY TEST

RING ON A STRING

Children sit in a circle, holding a long string in front of them tied at both ends. A ring or a polo mint has been slipped over the string before tying, and the players move their hands back and forth on the string, passing the ring from one player to another. One player stands in the centre and tries to guess who has the ring. The centre player can stop the passing at any stage and ask one of the passers to lift their hands. If the ring is in those hands, that player has to take the centre position.

RING ON A STRING

NAME IT

This is a game that will be thoroughly enjoyed by boys and girls. Draw all the letters of the alphabet on separate squares of paper or board, about 2 or 3 inch square, and put them in a hat or basin. Seat the children in front of you, so they can all see clearly the letters you pull out of the hat, which you take out one at a time quite indiscriminately. If you start the game with 'Fruits', the first person to name a fruit beginning with the letter you pull out – they are sure to shout it – gets the letter. When you have been right through the alphabet, see who has collected the most letters. Collect the letters to start again, and then play it with Animals, Birds, Towns, etc.

MURDER

Each player is given a slip of paper which no-one else is allowed to see. Two only of the slips have anything written on them. One reads 'Murderer', the other 'Detective'. The 'Detective' has to leave the room. The lights are turned out, and the crowd mixes up in the centre of the room, until the

Murderer puts his or her hands lightly around someone's throat. The person screams and falls to the ground. The lights are turned on, the Detective comes back into the room, and starts to question everyone, trying to find out who the Murderer is. All persons must answer truthfully any question the Detective asks, except the Murderer, who can tell any lie.

A warning on this game is that it could be rather a flop if you get a dull Detective. It may be better to choose the Detective rather than trust to the luck of the draw.

FIND MY NAME

This is an old game, but always a favourite. Also, adults must remember that what seems rather 'corny' to them, can be quite new to the growing boy or girl.

Have the names of a large number of famous men and women – sporting, political, historical, TV characters, etc. – printed on separate slips of paper. At the beginning pin one on the back of each guest without them seeing the name. The boys and girls then have to walk round talking to each other, trying to find out the name of the person printed on their own back by asking questions. The person to whom they are speaking must answer only 'Yes' or 'No' to their questions. As soon as a player has guessed one name, he or she goes back to the organizer, who transfers the slip of paper on to the front, and then pins another one on the back. The one who guesses the most after a certain length of time, about 20 minutes, or when all names have run out (whichever is sooner) is the winner.

UNTIE A PARCEL

Have a prize of some sort wrapped in layer on layer of brown paper, each layer tied with string, and each layer with a label printed on the outside. The labels will have written on them the following sort of things – 'For the girl with the brownest eyes', 'For the girl with the fairest hair', 'For the girl with the curliest hair', 'For the girl with the prettiest frock', 'For the boy with the longest legs', 'For the boy with the smartest tie', 'For the boy with the largest feet', 'For the boy with the longest eye-lashes', etc., etc.

Guests are all seated round in a circle and the parcel is

UNTIE A PARCEL

handed to one of them who reads the label on the outside, and hands it to the person he or she thinks it describes best. That player unwraps the outside layer, and reads the label underneath, pinned on the next layer of brown paper, and hands the parcel on again to whoever is thought fits the description. This continues until someone reaches the prize inside. Make a rule that no-one can have more than one turn until everybody has had one, so that you would have as many layers of brown paper as guests. (Or you could have two for each guest.)

8

MUSICAL GAMES

Musical games always go with a swing. They use up surplus energy without the children getting unruly, and they require little preparation on the part of the hostess.

A piano (with someone who can play it, of course), a radio, a record player or a cassette deck can all be used to provide the music, provided it can be stopped and started again quickly.

If the games are to be played outside, a drum or tin whistle could be used.

MUSICAL STATUES

This is always great fun. Players all dance or hop round the room to music, doing anything they like. As soon as the music stops, everyone must stand perfectly still, holding the position in which they are caught. Anyone moving at all until the music starts again, must drop out. The winner, of course, is the one left in last.

PASS THE PARCEL

Have a small prize of some sort wrapped in brown paper and tied with string, then wrapped in another layer of paper and tied again, and so on until it is a large parcel. Players sit

round in a circle and hand the parcel from hand to hand
while the music is playing. When it stops, whoever is holding
the parcel at that moment will undo the string and unwrap

the top layer of paper. The music will start again and the
parcel will start circulating again. As it gets smaller and
smaller, excitement will grow, each person who opens the
parcel hoping it is the last layer, and that he or she will get
the prize. This is the reverse of most musical games, in that
the players will want to be caught with the parcel rather
than get rid of it. You may have to make sure they don't
hang on to it.

POISONED HATS

Form everyone into a circle, and if there is a large number,
hand two or three old hats into the circle. These are to be

passed round from hand to hand while the music is played. When the music stops, anyone caught in possession of a hat is poisoned, and must drop out. When the group is reduced to only a few players, have only one hat in the ring. The last player to stay in is the winner.

MUSICAL NUMBERS

Have everyone walking round in a circle to music. When the music stops, the organizer will shout 'Four' or 'Six' or any number up to ten. All players instantly rush to form themselves into groups of the given number. If 'Five' is

called out, for example, everyone must form groups of five. Anyone left over drops out of the game, and marching starts again. Repeat with different numbers until only five or six players are left and then declare these the winners.

MUSICAL TELEPATHY

If no piano is available, this and the next game can be played by everyone humming or singing together loudly or softly, according to how the 'out' person is progressing.

One player leaves the room, and the rest decide on an action that person is to do, such as straightening a crooked rug, pulling down a blind, picking up a book that has fallen on the floor, etc. When he or she returns to the room, only the music will give a clue as to what is to be done. If that player approaches the spot where the action is to be performed the piano will play or the hummers hum loudly and fast. As the player moves away from it, the piano will play softly and slowly. If the player does something far away from the correct action it will play softly and slowly, but as he or she gets nearer the right thing, it will get louder and faster.

MUSICAL CLUE

This is similar to the above game, but instead of having to do some action, the person sent out of the room will have to find a peanut, thimble or some small object hidden. As the player gets near the object the piano will be played loudly, as he or she moves away from it, it will be played softly. This and the last game are only suitable for small parties.

POISONED CARPET

Players walk round in a circle to music. A small carpet is placed across the line of the circle at one spot, and all players have to walk on the mat when they come to it. The

person caught on the mat when the music stops each time has to drop out. The winner, of course, is the last one left in. If no one is on the mat when the music stops, the one nearest it must drop out.

MUSICAL CHAIRS

You need one chair less than the players for this game. Place the chairs in a line down the length of the room, facing one way, then the other alternately. While the music is playing, the players march in a circle round the chairs, and as soon as the music stops, everyone tries to sit down on a chair. One player, of course, will be left chairless. He or she drops

out of the game, one chair is taken from the end of the line, and the game goes on. Each time one person will miss out, and another chair will be taken away. When only two players are left, it is a good idea to have sentries, standing a few yards each side of the one remaining chair, around which the players have to walk. The one who gets the last chair is, of course, the winner.

MUSICAL ARMS

This is similar to the above game, except that you do not need chairs. Half the players, less one, stand in a line down the centre of the room, each one alternately putting a right or left hand on hip. The remaining players walk round them to music, grabbing an arm when the music stops. The one left without an arm drops out each time, and one of the 'arms' must also leave the line. When the game is finished, play it again with the 'arms' this time doing the marching round.

THE BLIND MUSICIAN

This is a variation of the well-known 'Hokey-Pokey'. Stand all players in a circle and blindfold one in the centre of the ring. Give this player a wand or baton of some sort – a pencil or rolled-up sheet of newspaper will do. All the players then have to walk round in a circle singing or humming some well-known tune. The blind musician will beat time with his baton. When the baton is dropped, everyone must stop. The blindfolded child will then point to one player, who has to sing the song alone. Disguising the voice is allowed, and the blind musician has to try and guess who it is. If successful he or she changes place with the musician. If unsuccessful, the player starts the singing again. If unsuccessful several times, have a change of musician after three guesses.

9

PENCIL AND PAPER GAMES

The only equipment required for the games in this section are a pencil and a piece of paper for each guest. They are thus very easy to prepare, and will keep boys and girls quiet. One should not, however, have too many pencil and paper games at one party, as some children find them boring.

DARK DRAWINGS

Give your guests a pencil and paper, then put out the light, and ask them to draw a lake. This sounds quite difficult and they will probably expect you to put on the light when they have finished. However, you then say, 'Now draw a boat on the water,' and 'Now draw a house on the shore.' Then ask for two men to be drawn in the boat, then a tree by the house, then oars in the men's hands, then a pier on the shore, then some clouds and the sun in the sky. Perhaps you would like to add a few more details. When finished, turn on the lights, and see what your artists have produced.

MODERN ART

Each player is given a piece of paper and a pencil, and is asked to draw a head and neck of any living creature.

Without letting anyone else see the result, the top of the paper is then folded over, so that only the lines of the neck

are showing. It is then handed on to the next player, who adds a body or trunk, leaving the top of the legs showing, and then handed to the next player. This last player adds the legs and feet. When the papers are unfolded and passed round, some very amusing 'works of art' are revealed.

BOOK SHAPES

Place about 12 books, of different sizes and colours, in a row, and allow your guests to look at them for about two or three minutes. Select books of varying height, width, and colour. Take the books away, and ask players to draw a picture of them as they stood in the row. They do not have to remember their titles or authors, but just the comparative sizes, and also to indicate what colour each was. This may sound easy, but it is amazing how hard it is to remember even half of them correctly.

CROSSWORDS

This is a game for older children which will require some careful thinking. It is based on the well-known crossword puzzle idea.

Give each player a pencil and a small piece of paper ruled into half-inch squares, as shown in the diagram:

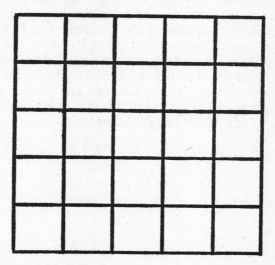

Each player in turn calls out a letter, and as a letter is called each player will write it in one of his squares, choosing whichever square thought best. When it comes to a player's turn to call one out he or she chooses a letter that will be most useful to him, helping to build on or complete a word. The object is to put the letters in the squares in such a position so that as many words as possible can be formed, reading both horizontally and vertically.

All letters called out must be put down somewhere, although they may not fit in with one's own words very well. When all the squares are filled, the players count up their words, and are awarded as many points for each word as there are letters in it. Words within words do not count, nor do proper names.

APT DESCRIPTIONS

Everyone is given two slips of paper. On one slip guests must write their names, and on the other they are asked to give a detailed description of the appearance and habits of any animal they choose, without giving its name. The names are then collected in one hat and the animal descriptions in another. These are then handed round to the guests again, each one taking a slip from each hat; and reading out, in turn what is found on the slips. In each case there will be the name of one of the people present with a very amusing description.

NAME THE SHOPS

This is a game for older children, and could only be played where you were sure all the guests would be familiar with a particular street.

Give each player a pencil and piece of paper and, naming a particular section of a well-known street, ask them to write down all the shops in that section in their correct

order. The first and last shop would need to be given as a
guide. Part of a well-known high street, situated between
two other streets, is probably the best to give. But you want
to make sure your guests are old enough to have been into
town regularly to do this.

SIX OF A KIND

Give each guest a pencil and piece of paper, and ask them
to divide their paper into six columns. At the top of each
column ask them to write the name of a different category,
as you call them out. 'Car' at the top of one, for example,
then 'Bird', 'Flower', 'City', 'Girl's Name', 'Boy's Name',
'Tree', 'Animal', or whatever categories you prefer.

Then call out a letter, such as 'M', and ask players to
write down an example of each category, in its appropriate
column, beginning with the letter 'M'. For example, a car
commencing with 'M', in the 'Car' column, etc. After a
short space of time, go round the circle, asking each guest
to read out his six names. Anyone having the same one as
someone else, crosses it off the list. The player with the most
names not put down by any other player wins the game.
Do not play this game with too large a party, as it takes too
long to go round the circle. If guests are enjoying it, it can
be repeated several times with different letters.

CONCOCT A SENTENCE

Give all boys and girls a pencil and paper. Then ask each
one in turn to call out a word – any word they choose. As
they call them out, all players will write them down on

their sheets of paper. If you find everyone is naming a noun of some sort – cow, ship, boy, etc. – you should say to the next one, 'Make yours a verb'. In this way make sure there are some verbs, and possibly a couple of adjectives also, among the words called out. When everyone has named a word, and these are all written down, then tell players that each one has to make up a sentence out of the words on the sheet of paper. Do not tell them what they have to do with the words before naming them.

After about ten minutes, or less, if most guests are finished, have them read out their sentences, and give prizes for the best.

WORD-MAKING

Choose some long word, such as 'Hippopotamus', or 'Rhododendron', or some word that will have particular association for those present, such as the name of their school (if suitable) or of the village or suburb in which they live. Give guests a pencil and paper and ask them to write the word on the top. They then have to see how many words they can write down made up from the key-word. For example, from 'Hippopotamus', hit, hip, his, stop, mat, past, map, stamp, etc. could be made. Words must be at least three letters. The same letters can be used over and over again in different words, but if there is only one of a certain letter in the key-word, then this can be used only once in any one word derived from it.

OBSTINATE ARTISTS

This is an excellent competition and very amusing, and is recommended mainly for older boys and girls.

Give guests a plain piece of paper and pencil, and ask them to illustrate the *name* of a well known film. It must be made quite clear that the contents or story of the film are not to be illustrated, but just the *title* of it. For example, 'Jaws' could be illustrated by a great mouthful of teeth, or 'Grease' by a tin fallen on its side with grease coming out of it. The different drawings are then collected, numbered, and put in a row for the guests to guess, each competitor going round looking at each other's drawings and writing down the numbers and titles as they guess them. A prize could be given for the most guessed by any competitor, or the drawing voted most amusing. It must be stressed that no drawing ability is needed for this competition, and often the funniest and most successful illustrations are the worst drawn. It is the IDEA that counts and not the drawing.

OBSERVATION TEST

Send one or more guests out of the room. Supply the remaining ones with pencil and paper, and ask them to describe the clothes of the person or persons sent out of the room. Give one point for each detail remembered, such as colour of tie, suit, shoes, dress, etc., or type of coat, collar, shoe, etc. But take off two points for any detail given wrongly. Then find the winner by totalling the points. Don't, of course, tell the guests what they are to write before sending the guinea-pig players outside, and you will find that some people will not have noticed any details at all.

HOW MANY?

Give all guests a pencil and piece of paper, and ask them to write down all the things they can see in the room beginning with a certain letter. If, for example, you say 'B', they could possibly put book, book-shelf, beading, beads (on the guests), bracket, etc. Or for 'C', they could write chair, cushion, clock, cupboard, container, etc. This can be played several times, finding a winner each time.

QUESTION AND ANSWER

Give all players a slip of paper and pencil each, and then divide them into two groups. One half of those present have to think of a difficult situation and write it down in the form of the following question: 'What would you do if

...... (putting in the difficult situation) ...... ?' The other half of the players have to write answers to such unknown situations: 'I would ...... (Putting in a suggestion as to what they would do) ......' The slips are dropped into two hats, one for the problems and one for the answers. One slip is then drawn from each hat at a time, and the problem and answer read out. Some ridiculous and amusing combinations will result.

10

NO PREPARATION NECESSARY

For the games in this section, no preparation on the'part of the hostess is necessary. They are not the most exciting or amusing games in the book, but they are very handy to know. Parents should have this section in the book well marked, so that they can refer to it quickly if they find the programme is finishing too soon.

Several of the musical games in chapter 8 can also be played without any previous preparation, provided a piano or record player is available, whilst chapter 9 gives a number of very excellent games that can be used if a plentiful supply of pencils and paper is available.

PERCOLATE

This is an amusing variation of the usual sort of guessing game. One person goes out of the room, and the others choose a verb such as 'walking', 'knitting', 'singing', etc.

The person outside comes back and tries to guess the word by asking one question of everyone in turn, but in asking the questions, the word 'percolate' must be used in place of the word trying to be guessed. For example, if the word chosen were 'walk', the question would be 'Do you percolate each day?' and the answer would be 'Yes'. If the question were 'Do I percolate?' the answer would be 'Yes'. To 'Does one percolate with one's mouth?' the answer would be 'No'. 'Do I percolate with the lower half of my body?' will bring the answer 'Yes', and so on until the player guesses the word. Players must answer only 'Yes' or 'No'.

FIND THE LEADER

Players stand in a circle, and one player goes out. A leader is appointed, and then all start clapping, until the person outside comes in. The leader then changes actions; for

example, from clapping to rubbing the nose, to hopping, to singing, to waving an arm, etc., and everyone has to follow. The person in the centre has to find out who the leader is, and it is amazing how difficult it can be. All players should not watch the leader, as the action will quickly go round the circle. When finally discovered, the leader goes out for the next round, and a new leader is appointed.

HA! HA! HA!

Players sit round in a circle. The first player says 'Ha!', the second 'Ha! Ha!', the third 'Ha! Ha! Ha!', and so on, each player saying one more 'Ha!' than the one before. No one must smile or laugh while saying the 'Ha's!', but must speak them as deliberately and seriously as possible. Anyone who smiles or gets the number of Ha's wrong is out. Others, however, can laugh as much as they like, until it is their turn.

LAUGHING HANDKERCHIEF

All players, except one, stand in a circle. That one stands inside the circle and tosses a handkerchief into the air. That player then starts laughing. Everyone must also laugh, until the handkerchief touches the floor, when there must be perfect silence. Anyone laughing after the handkerchief touches the floor or stopping laughing before it touches the floor is out, and must leave the circle.

LAUGHING HAT

An alternative of the above is to have the players standing or sitting in two lines. The centre player throws up an old hat. If it lands on its crown, one side of players laughs, if it lands on its brim, the other side laughs. Anyone laughing out of turn has to drop out.

LAUGHING HANDKERCHIEF

CONSECUTIVE TOWNS

All players sit in a circle. One says the name of a town, and the person sitting next has to name a city or town beginning with the letter that ended the city just named. For example, the first player may say 'Edinburgh', the next could say 'Hastings', the next 'Swindon', the next 'Newport', the next 'Tunbridge Wells', etc. If a player cannot carry on, and someone else can, then the person who fails drops out. The same town cannot be named twice.

EARTH, WATER, AIR

Players sit in a circle with someone in the centre. The person in the centre points at one of the other players and shouts either 'Earth', 'Air', 'Fire', or 'Water' and counts to ten, If 'Earth' is called the player must name an animal; if 'Air'. a bird must be named; if 'Water' a fish must be named. This must be done before the count of ten, or the player must take the centre position. If 'Fire' is called the player pointed at must remain silent.

This game can be played alternatively by a ball or knotted handkerchief being thrown to the person who has to respond. The same animal, fish or bird cannot be named twice.

GOING TO MARKET

Players sit in a circle. The first one says, 'I went to market, and bought a pound of butter', The next one says, 'I went to market and I bought a pound of butter and an apple'. The third one repeats what the second one said, adding another article such as 'a fan', or 'a cat', or 'a cauliflower'. As it goes round the circle each player has to repeat all the things already bought, and then add another article. Anyone missing out an article drops out.

GRANDMA'S FOOTSTEPS

One player (or an adult – it can be a real grandma!) stands well in front of the rest of the party, to whom his or her back is turned. All other players try to creep up. As soon as she turns round they must stand perfectly still. If she sees anyone moving, or if they cannot hold their position while she is watching, they go back to the beginning. The winner is the one who touches grandma first without being caught. The game may end here or else this player then takes the position of grandma. Alternatively, the player in front can hold a present of 'treasure' behind the back, which the ones creeping up try to grab.

POISONED SPOT

Players form a ring holding hands. In the centre of the ring you can either draw a circle of a few feet in diameter, or

GRANDMA'S FOOTSTEPS

else place two or three cushions. The circle or the cushions are said to be poisoned, and the idea is for players to keep away from them and to pull other players on to them. Anyone touching either the circle or the cushion falls out. The winner, of course, is the one left in last. Make sure players do not let go of each other's hands, as this will prevent the game from getting too rough. Make a rule that anyone dropping hands until someone is forced on to the poisoned spot, must drop out.

11

RACES

All children love races, and they always provide a great deal of fun. Collected together in this chapter is a great variety of this sort of entertainment. The races range from the very simple sort, probably already known to you, to more complicated ones. They include races for individuals, pairs, and teams, so everyone should find something that appeals to them.

The first section is a mixture, including some very amusing ones. Then come sections on team races, individual races, and races that can be used either for teams or individuals (everyone competing for himself).

BONNET RACE

This will cause a great deal of amusement. Divide your guests into teams and provide an old-fashioned bonnet, the type tied with ribbons or strings, for each team. At the word 'Go', the first member in each team puts on the bonnet and ties a bow under the chin. The second player in the team then unties the bow, takes the bonnet off the first player, and puts it on his own head, tying the bow again. The third player does the same thing, and so on down the line. First team finished wins. Players should be warned that each must tie the bow before the next in the team touches it.

BONNET RACE

DRESS THE MODEL

Again divide guests into teams, and supply each team with a suitcase, containing a similar collection of clothing – hat, gloves, shoes, scarf, coat, umbrella, etc. There should be the same number of articles of clothing (less one) as members in a team. Each team then selects a model who has to stand at the other end of the room. At a given signal, the teams open their suitcases, and one player runs up with one article of clothing and puts it on the model. On returning to the line, the next player rushes off with the next article. The model must stand rigid and not assist the players in any way.

A second contest can be run by taking these clothes off the model and returning them to the suitcase. But don't forget the point at which you commenced dressing the model!

BLIND FEEDERS

Divide the players into pairs, and blindfold them. Give both players of each pair a spoon and a saucer with about a dozen shelled peanuts in it. The pairs then feed each other the peanuts. Although the race will go to the quickest, the number of peanuts spilt in the process should also be taken into account. You could make a rule that anyone spilling more than three is disqualified.

BACK-TO-BACK RACE

Divide the children into pairs. Each pair stands back to back and the two players link arms. They then have to run to a line and back again, so that one player runs forward and the other other backward. On the way back this will be reversed. This causes a lot of fun.

SPOON CONTEST

Divide the players into pairs, and give each pair a dish of ice-cream between them and two spoons tied together with a string about 6 inches long. Using the tied spoons, the contestants have to see which pair can finish their ice-cream first.

SPELLING RELAY RACE

Divide guests into teams, and place stacks of letters (one
stack for each team) on a table at one end of the room.
The M.C. then calls out a long word. The first player runs
up, finds the first letter of the word, lays it face upwards
on the table, and returns to his place. The second player
finds the second letter, etc., until the word is spelt. If the
word is longer than the number of players in the team, some
members can run up twice.

APPLES ON STRING

For this contest you need a rope or cross piece of timber
supported between two side-posts, several yards apart.
From the rope or cross piece, tie about half a dozen apples.
Players are lined up and started. They race to the apples and
try to bite them. The one who gets three bites first wins. You
will probably need to run this in heats and supply fresh
apples each time. Children are not allowed to use their
hands.

APPLES ON STRING

TEAM RACES

In the following races, the teams are lined up, but members do not move from their places. They hand or pass articles from player to player in the team.

PIN RACE

Players cross their wrists, gripping the left wrist of their neighbour with their own right hand. At the head of each line is a small pile of pins, and these have to be passed down, one at a time, by the left hands, from one player to the next.

TOOTH-PICK RACE

Players hold a toothpick in their mouths, and a ring has to be passed down the line by means of these toothpicks. Players may not use their hands.

MATCH-BOX RACE

Each player in turn holds the outside part of a match box on their noses, and must transfer it from one nose to that of the next member of the team, without using hands.

NECKTIE RACE

Each player in turn must tie a necktie around their neck, then untie it, and pass it on.

PARCEL RACE

A brown-paper parcel tied with string is handed to the first player, who unwraps it, and passes paper, string and object on to the next in the team. This player wraps the parcel up again, and passes it on to the next player, who again unwraps it, and so on down the line.

INDIVIDUAL RACES

The following races are suitable only for players to compete separately against each other. In some cases it may be necessary to have heats, the winners competing in the final.

POLO RACE

This is strongly recommended. Polos, or any sweets with a hole in the middle are tied on the end of longish pieces of cotton, all the same length, and one is given to each player. Players put the loose end of the cotton in their mouths, and try to chew up the cotton until they can get the polo in their mouths.

STREAMER RACE

Players have to cut or tear up the centre of a narrow piece of tape or paper streamer. If either half of the tape is broken, the player is disqualified. This idea can be used to have a race in *pairs*, by giving each pair a narrow piece of paper (part of a paper streamer) about 20 feet long, or the width of the room. The pair has to tear it down the centre, one commencing at each end of the streamer.

MINT RACE

Players are each given a mint or similar sweet. After eating the sweet, the race starts. Players take the paper in which the sweet was wrapped, and start tearing a narrow piece from round the edge, not breaking it off, and gradually nearing the centre, with the strip getting longer and longer. The player with the longest piece, after a given time, wins.

NEWSPAPER RACE

Give each player two sheets of newspaper. They have to race by stepping on to the newspapers only. Thus a player has to put down one of his sheets, step on to it, put down the other sheet, step on it, reach back to get the first sheet and move it forward, and so on until the finishing line is reached.

BRICK OR FLOWERPOT RACE

A race similar to the newspaper race (above), can be run by giving each player two or three bricks or flowerpots. They must race, stepping only on the bricks or flowerpots, and not touching the ground with either feet or hands. If they touch the ground or overbalance, they must go back to the starting point.

POTATO RACE

Each contestant is given a wastepaper basket or bucket. In front stretches a row of four or five potatoes or tennis balls, placed a yard or two apart. Each player has to run forward, pick up the first potato, run back, and put it in the basket. Each player then has to collect the second, third, fourth, etc., each one separately. When all have been collected, the player picks up the basket with the potatoes in it, and runs to the finishing line. The player can start with the first or last potato.

SACK RACE

Players all have to run with their feet in a sack. Make sure that all sacks are of similar size and texture, so that everyone has an equal chance. The race can be started with competitors either standing up, or lying on their backs. If the latter, they have to get up on the word 'Go', without touching the ground with their hands.

OBSTACLE RACE

This is always fun. Arrange any sort of course with a lot of hazards on the way – players have to go over seats, under a net, eat an apple on a string, skip for some distance, etc. It is necessary to have room or equipment for all to do each stage at once. It is not fair if obstacles allow only one

SACK RACE

competitor to get through, or over, at a time. This means
that the child who gets there first will get an almost unbeat-
able lead on the others, as the ones following will have to
wait while the first one surmounts the obstacles. Make sure
all runners understand the course and what they have to do
before they start.

INDIVIDUAL OR RELAY RACES

The following races can be run as either individual or relay races.

Individual Races

If you decide on individual races, it is best to have heats, with five or six in each heat, the winners then competing against each other in the final. Children are used to doing this at school, so there should be no trouble in organizing it. Make sure there are no delays, however. The onlookers, waiting for their heat, will enjoy watching the other heats, but may grow noisy if they have to wait too long. Most children prefer to be doing something, rather than watching.

[Relay Races]

You may prefer to run them as Relay Races, which have the decided advantage of occupying everyone at the same time. Divide the company into teams of equal numbers, and line them up at one end of the room or lawn. One player in each team carries out the required action, whatever it is, and then returns. Then the next player does likewise. A player must not start until the previous player is back in position, and the team wins in which all players finish first. Make it clear that any team will be disqualified if one member starts to run before the one in front is back in place.

PEANUT AND FORK RACE

Players have to carry an unshelled peanut on a fork the length of the room. Start them with fork in hand and peanut on floor in front of them. The peanut has to be picked up

with the fork without competitors' touching the nut with their fingers. If they drop the nut while running they must once again pick it up with the fork. Make sure all peanuts are much the same size and shape.

PEA AND STRAW RACE

Players have to carry a pea by breathing in (sucking) action, on the end of a drinking straw. Start them standing upright, with straw in mouth, and the pea on the floor in front of them.

TOOTHPICKS AND PEANUTS

Players have to push an unshelled peanut across the floor with a toothpick. Once again make sure that all peanuts are a similar size and shape.

LIGHT A CANDLE RACE

Players have to light a candle and carry it alight to the finishing line. If it goes out they must return to the start and light it again. Best played outdoors on a calm day, as this could be a fire risk inside.

BALL AND BALLOON

Supply each player with a ping-pong bat or tennis racket and a balloon. They must hit the ballon through the air to the finishing line. If it falls to the ground either on the way or at the finish, they must start again.

BURSTING RACE

Players have to run to the end of the room and burst a balloon or paper bag. They must not start blowing up the balloon or bag until they reach a given place – either a line drawn across the room or the opposite wall.

WHISTLE AND EAT

Players have to run to the end of the room or lawn, eat a biscuit, then whistle a tune. Do not give them the biscuits until they reach the end or line to which they are running. The biscuits could be either handed to them then or placed in a row on the ground there.

MARBLE RACE

Players have to carry a marble on two pencils or felt-tip pens. Start them with the pencils in hand and the marbles on the floor, and have them pick up the marbles without touching them with their hands. Make sure they hold the marble at some distance from the fingers when running, and do not use their fingers or thumbs to balance the marbles.

SWEEPING RACE

Each player has a small whisk or broom, and has to sweep a piece of paper the length of the room.

BALL AND PLATE RACE

Stretch a piece of string across one end of the room, about five feet high and two or three feet out from the end wall. Each player has to balance a soft ball on a plate up to the line, toss the ball over the string and catch it on the other side. If they lose the ball they have to start from the beginning again.

ORANGE ON A SPOON

Players have to hop, while carrying an orange on a large spoon. Start them standing on one leg, with spoon in hand, and orange on the floor in front of them. They then have to pick up the orange with the spoon without touching the ground with their hands or their second foot.

DRAGGING THE ORANGE

An orange is placed on a square of cardboard, to which is attached a long piece of string. Each player has to drag the orange along on the piece of board by pulling the string. If the orange rolls off, players have to go back to the beginning.

ORANGE ON A SPOON

BLOWING RACE

Players have to blow a feather, a balloon, or a ping-pong
ball the length of the room.

LEMON AND PENCIL RACE

A lemon has to be rolled by a pencil in the player's hand.

BLOWING RACE

CHERRY RACE

Players carry a cherry on the back of one of their hands.

LEMONADE BOTTLES

Players have to roll a lemonade bottle across the floor with a narrow stick. It is harder than it sounds.

LEMONADE BOTTLES

12

PLANNING A SPECIAL PARTY

Though it is generally true that children's parties need not
be a great deal of work you may feel like making some extra
effort, and giving a 'special' party.

There are all sorts of ways a party can be made special.
It may involve something unusual or expensive in the way
of catering or entertainment, or a special gift may be given
to each guest. Such things, however, are not essential to a
successful party, and, even if they can be afforded, can
easily give an unnecessary impression of ostentation.

The best way to make a party 'special' is by extra effort
and originality on the part of the parent. Arranging such a
party can be lots of fun. One good way is to have it based
on a motif or theme. Select a subject such as 'Ships' or
'Pirates' or 'Horses' and have the subject selected featured in
all aspects of the party – invitations, decorations, hats, bags
of sweets, games, and food.

This, of course, means work. It also requires more
thought and planning than an ordinary party. It will almost
certainly involve your making the hats, sweet-bags, invitations, etc., yourself, as you are very unlikely to be able
to buy them to fit in with the theme. Fortunately, none of
these things is difficult to make, and they can be lots of fun,
but it does require time, planning and thought.

Select the Theme
First of all, you must decide on the subject of the party. For
example, you may think a 'Ship Party' would be a good idea,
and everything must then be designed around ships.

Design a Motif

Having selected the subject matter, the next step is to design a motif or pattern which can be used throughout. The best idea is to get a good outline of some ship – yacht, liner, galleon or anything readily recognizable in outline.

You want to be able to cut it out in board or paper (without the necessity of adding any lines to it afterwards), so that it shows quite clearly, *in silhouette*, what it is. That will make your job much easier. If you cannot draw, and few of us can, look through magazines, newspapers or children's books till you find something you can copy.

Of course, it need not be the same motif throughout. You could have three or four different types of ships, but the average person will probably find it much easier to concentrate on one.

Cut Your Guides

Once you have designed your motif, you want to draw or trace it on to a fairly thick board, probably in two or three sizes – say, a very small one, a large one and one between. Then cut the shapes out of the board and you have patterns ready for drawing the outline of the motifs or designs to go on anything needed for the party. You merely place the cardboard shape on white or coloured paper, or on board that you are using. Go round the outline of the pattern in pencil, and thus you have the design all ready for use on either hat, card, invitation or whatever you desire.

Paint or Cut Out

You can either draw the design in this way straight on to whatever you are decorating and then paint it, or you can draw it on coloured board, cut out the resultant design and stick it on to the various party objects.

The latter is probably the better. It is easier, and brighter colours can be obtained with more even results – unless you are very expert in the use of paints.

Pictures

An alternative to designing and cutting out or drawing a

motif, is to collect, from magazines and children's picture books, numbers of small pictures dealing with the subject of the party, such as ships or horses. In some cases, this could prove rather difficult, and also rather expensive, although you will note that we recommend it at a later stage for 'Nursery Rhyme' and 'Christmas' parties.

Invitations

There are several different ways of making your invitations.

Just a plain sheet of white paper can be used with the motif or picture stuck to the top centre or one of the top corners of the sheet, and the invitation printed, written or typed below. Alternatively, a sheet of white paper can be folded, the motif or picture placed on the outside, and the invitation put inside.

A different type altogether is to make the whole invitation in the shape of the motif. Place your largest pattern on a piece of coloured board, say bright blue for a 'Ship' party, outline it in pencil, cut out the shape, then write or paste the words of the invitation on to the shape.

Another similar idea is to fold a piece of thin board in two, and outline the motif on to it, leaving a small area of the design at the left hand side which will remain uncut. Then cut out the shape so that you can have it double, but joined at the centre. The shape can then be sent to guests closed. They will open it out and find the invitation written inside. I have seen this done most effectively.

If you like hand-work you can print the invitation neatly on each card. A good idea to save this is to have the words typed, preferably on an electric typewriter so that it looks a bit like print, on small pieces of paper, the right size to fit neatly on to the shape. These typed invitations can then be easily pasted on to the board.

Wording of the Invitation

Formal invitations, such as are used for other social events, are very seldom used for children's parties. A very informal invitation along the following lines is better:

'I am having a party on
.... (date), and would like
you to come'

or

'We would like to see you at ....
(name of host or hostess) place for a
party (or birthday party), on .... (date)'

or

'Please come to my party
on .... (date)'
etc., etc.

For a special party, however, the wording should be altered
and made more unconventional in order to fit in with the
spirit of the day. For our Ship Party, for example, you could
say something like:

'Ship ahoy!
Come on, you Landlubbers!
.... (Name of Host) is having a
Ship Party on .... (date) at the
S.S. .... (name of house). Let us
know if you will be coming aboard.'

This is only a suggestion. It could be made longer or shorter
or more formal or more boisterous. It will depend on your
ideas and individuality and the guests you intend to
invite.

So much for the invitations. Send them out along these
lines, and I shall be very surprised if you do not get some
amusing replies.

Hats
Once again considerable pleasure, fun and ingenuity can go
into the making of these.

One of the easiest ways is a narrow strip of thin board,
about 1½ to 2 inches wide, cut the length to fit a child's head,
and fastened at the back with glue, a few stitches, a
staple, or a piece of sticky tape. The party motif, for example, the ship, would then be cut out of stiff coloured
board and stuck to the front of the headband. One of the

prettiest hats I have ever seen on a little girl was a hat of this sort with a silver star fastened in front. In her party frock, the little girl looked just like a little fairy. These are very easy to make and yet most effective.

Crepe Paper Hats

Another pretty type of hat that can be easily made is with coloured crepe paper. Cut a piece of paper wide enough to go round a child's head (cutting so that the stretch of the crepe paper goes *round* the head), and about 9 or 12 inches high, according to what style of hat you want. It is a good idea to vary the style. Fold the pieces over and machine them down the side. Fold about one inch up round the bottom to make a band. There are different ways to treat the top. Here are three simple suggestions:

(1) Machine across it, and then sew paper streamers on to each top corner.

(2) Cut it up and down in points to look like a crown.

(3) Gather it to a point at the top, and fasten it about 2 inches down from the top with cotton first, then with paper streamers. Then cut down the two inches above the streamers into a fringe.

When you have finished the hats paste the motifs, cut out of thin board, on the front of each one. Do not try to cut the motifs out of crepe paper. It will not stand up, and crepe paper is difficult to stick satisfactorily on to crepe paper.

When cutting streamers out of crepe paper, always cut them along the length of the roll of paper, as they then crinkle attractively. If cut across the width of the paper they will hang stiffly and be harder to manage.

One last and very easy suggestion for making the hats to fit your party theme, is to buy some of the very simple plain ones, made out of crepe paper, that are usually available at chain stores, and then fasten your motif on the front of each one.

Sweet Bags

This last suggestion is also the easiest way to make the bags
or baskets for sweets fit into your party. Buy the cheap plain
ones and then paste the motif on the front of the handle of
each.

Another very easy way is to place the sweets in squares of
cellophane, gather the cellophane around the sweets and tie
it a few inches from the top. Then stick the motif to the
outside or tie it on.

It is also quite simple to make baskets out of thin cardboard. Cut pieces about nine inches square, then fold them
in half four times, so that when opened out you get 16
squares as illustrated:

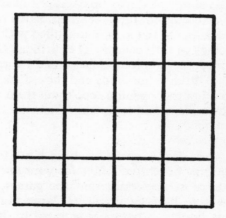

On two opposite sides, slit the corner squares to the first
crease. These corner squares are then folded over and pasted
on to the two end centre squares, forming the ends of the
basket. Handles about one half-inch wide and five or six
inches long should also be cut out and pasted in position
with the cut-out motif finally added to the outside.

Place-Cards

Place-cards, put at each place with guests's name written on
them can also be made to fit in with the theme. Buy or cut

out small cards and stick a tiny motif on one side, or else
cut larger pieces of white board, about four inches square,
fold along the centre, so they will stand at each place, then
stick or draw the motif on the front with the name written
beside it.

Balloons
If you want to be really energetic you can blow the balloons
up in the morning and paint the motifs on to them with
ordinary water colours.

Catering
The food also of course should be made to fit in with the
theme of your party. For a Ship Party, biscuits can be made
and cut in the shape of ships. Boat-shaped cakes can have
paper sails standing in their centres. Savouries can be
bought or made in the shape of boats, filled with cheese and
a paper sail stuck in their centres. The Birthday Cake should
have a ship for its centrepiece. Cakes could be iced with the
shape of a ship done in hundreds and thousands. This is not
a recipe book, but the ingenious cook will think of numbers
of ways to make her food look 'ship-like'.

Games
Although a great deal of space has been given to describing
how to make the decorative things for your special party it
is, of course, most important that the games also fit the
theme. This is really very simple. A large number of the
games in this book can be easily adapted to fit a different
theme.

Sometimes all you need do is to alter the name. Other
times you alter slightly what is to be done, or how it is to be
done. Once you get the idea you will find yourself thinking
of a host of different ways for making games fit your theme.

For example, the following are some games already
described in this book, which you could alter to use in a
Ship Party.

The musical game called 'Poisoned Carpet' described on
page 58, could be called 'Man Overboard'. Guests could be

told that the small piece of carpet is the sea, and that the person caught on it when the music stops has fallen overboard, is drowned, and is therefore out. The game 'Dark Drawings' on page 61, could be played. Instead of asking guests to draw a lake, ask them to draw a steamer. Then say: 'Now draw the Captain on the bridge', 'Now add a lifeboat', 'Draw a seagull hovering near the ship', 'Draw smoke coming out of its funnels', etc., etc. 'Make an Elephant', on page 44, could be adapted, calling it 'Make a Ship'.

'Hokey-Pokey', as described on page 30, could be played, calling it 'Ship Hokey-Pokey', and players having to say 'Ship Ahoy or 'All Aboard', instead of 'Hokey-Pokey', while 'King Neptune' described on page 31, under the heading of 'Pussy Wants a Home', would be another suitable game. 'Memory Test' on page 48, could be adapted, putting only those articles on the tray that have some connection with the sea or ships, and the Polo Race, described on page 85, would be very apt.

So one could go on. Look through the pages of this book and you will find plenty of ideas for games that can fit in with 'Ships'.

In the next chapter are a number of other themes that could be used for special parties.

13

THEMES FOR SPECIAL PARTIES

The last chapter dealt in considerable detail with how to plan a special party, applying the same theme and motif to all the different aspects of a children's party. In the following pages are a number of ideas and themes that can be applied along these lines.

In each case the main theme only is given, with a few general ideas for games, decoration, etc. There is no attempt to describe the parties fully. This is, firstly, because the games you choose, and the way in which you adapt certain games to fit your theme, will vary according to the age and type of children for whom you are catering. Secondly, once you begin to think in terms of having, say, a 'Horse Party', or a 'Nursery Rhyme Party', or a 'Pirate Party', you will immediately find ideas flocking into your head to supplement the ideas and suggestions given below.

Also, we must stress again that this is not a recipe book. Where we give ideas for food decoration to fit in with any particular theme, it is a suggestion as regards appearance, shape or organization only. Details of recipes will be found in the dozens and dozens of excellent recipe books already produced.

Below then are some suggestions you may find helpful for a 'special' party. It will be immediately clear which are most suitable for boys and which for girls.

A FAIRY PARTY

A fairy party is a theme that would bring great delight to little girls. Design a motif in the shape of a fairy for invitations, etc., or alternatively, use a tinselled or silver star, which would probably be easier. To make the various things suggested below use either silver board, or sprinkle silver spangles or tinsel on cardboard, sticking them with glue.

For each guest, make a fairy wand out of a thin stick, with a silver star stuck or tacked to one end; a hat with a silver star stuck in front; and a pair of small silver wings that can be pinned on the back. Give the guests these as they arrive (thus departing from the usual procedure of giving the hats at tea time), and let the little girls play fairies for a while. They will love it.

Other games they could play are 'Find Your Pair', on page 25, calling it 'Fairy Circles'; 'Cat and Mouse', on page 28, calling it 'Fairies and Goblins', the player trying to get into the circle being a wicked goblin.

'Hokey-Pokey' on page 30, using one of the fairy words instead of a rolled-up newspaper; 'Ring on a String', on page 49, calling it 'The Magic Ring'; 'Poisoned Carpet', on page 58 calling it 'The Magic Carpet', and saying that the player caught on the carpet is bewitched and is therefore 'out'; 'Word Making', on page 66, using 'Fairyland' as the keyword, etc., etc.

Be lavish with silver tinsel, silver paper, spangles, etc., in decorating the table and cakes, and a lovely effect will be obtained.

A PIRATE PARTY

Make either a skull and cross-bones or a treasure chest your motif throughout. A hat with a skull and cross-bones in white stuck on it, and a black patch with string attached to each side to be tied over one eye, distributed to each child on arrival, would cause a lot of fun. If you feel equal to it, you could add a long cardboard sword or short cardboard dagger. They would not cause any harm, but would be sure to result in considerable noise and action. They would certainly be appreciated.

Alternatively, have the hat and eye-patch at each place at the party table. Give the sweets to each child in small boxes marked 'Treasure Chest'.

Suggestions for games that would fit in with the theme are 'Great grey-green greasy Limpopo', described on page 25, entitled 'Pirates' Island', the part marked out being a pirates' island; 'Cat and Mouse', on page 28, called 'The

A PIRATE PARTY

Navy is After You', the one on the outside being a naval ship trying to get to a pirate ship inside, the rest of the pirates trying to stop it; 'What's the time, Mr. Wolf?' on page 29 adapted the same way, Mr. Wolf being a naval vessel and the rabbits being pirates; an ordinary peanut hunt, called a 'Treasure Hunt'; 'Twos and Threes', on page 32, to be called 'Pirate Chase', the circles into which the hunted escape from the hunters being known as 'safe', or 'secret ports'; 'Rob the Shop', on page 22, called 'Race for Treasure'; or 'Tom Tiddler's Ground', on page 22, called 'Treasure Trove'; 'Ring on a String', on page 49, called 'Find the Treasure'; 'Pass the Parcel', on page 54, called 'Musical Treasure'; 'Poisoned Carpet', on page 58, entitled 'Walking the Plank', the carpet being the plank, and anyone caught on it 'out'; 'Poisoned Spot', on page 75, altered the same way; etc., etc.

A COPS AND ROBBERS PARTY

This is another theme guaranteed to delight the heart of children. Design a motif to go on hats, invitations, place-cards, etc., in the shape of a gun, handcuffs, or a police-man's helmet. Alternatively, you may be able to buy policeman's toy helmets for all guests, and if you presented these to them on arrival, plus guns and handcuffs made from cardboard, they would have a wonderful time playing with them. It would, of course, be rather boisterous.

There are a host of games that could be played to fit in with the theme. 'Great grey-green greasy Limpopo', on page 25; 'Cat and Mouse', on page 28; 'What's the Time Mr. Wolf?', on page 29; 'Fox and Geese', page 32; 'Twos and

Threes', page 32; could all have their names altered to fit
the central idea, and be played with the chaser or catcher
in each instance called the 'cop', and the pursued or caught
called the 'robbers'. 'Poisoned Carpet', on page 58 and
'Poisoned Spot', on page 75, could be altered so that the
poisoned places were called 'prison' in each case, and the
person 'out' a 'caught robber'. Any of the many team races
given in Chapter 11 would also be very suitable, one team
of 'cops' competing against another team of 'robbers'.

A COWBOY PARTY

A 'Cowboy' party, similar to the 'Cops and Robbers' one
described above, would also be very popular, and could be
just as easily organized. The motif for hats, invitations, etc.,
could be a Cowboy's stetson or a gun. If, on arrival, cowboy

hats and cardboard guns were given to half the guests, and Red Indian head-dresses to the other half, they could have a wonderful time playing 'Cowboys and Indians'. If you think this too boisterous an idea, as I personally would, keep the hats until party-time, but it would still be an attractive idea to have one half Cowboys and the other half Indians. The hats could be either bought or made.

All the games recommended for the 'Cops and Robbers' party would fit in just as well for a 'Cowboy' party, one side being 'Cowboys' and the other side 'Indians'.

A CHRISTMAS PARTY

The motif designed for invitations, hats, baskets, etc., could be the simple outline of a Christmas Tree, or the more difficult shape of Father Christmas's head done in red board, with a dab of white cotton wool stuck on for his beard. An alternative suggestion is to collect small Christmas pictures, of which there are always plenty, from magazines, newspapers, last year's Xmas cards, and use these to stick on invitations, etc. One last suggestion is that, if you have access to a holly tree, use small sprigs of holly for decorations. If you cut two small slits in the board for invitations, place-cards, baskets, etc., the stem of the holly can be threaded through these and kept in place.

Decorations for the food, table, etc., should carry out the Christmas idea in the same way, and below are suggestions for games.

'Rob the Shop' on page 22, or 'Tom Tiddler's Ground' on page 22 could be played with the small presents wrapped in Christmas paper; 'Tommy Tucker' on page 27 could be called 'Christmas Dinner', the centre player saying 'Run for your Christmas dinner'; 'Posting Letters' on page 36 could be changed to 'Posting Christmas Cards'; 'Make an Elephant' on page 44 could be turned into 'Make Father Christmas'; 'Memory Test' on page 48 would appeal to children if it were called 'Father Christmas's Tray' and all the objects small toys; 'Untie a Parcel', page 52, 'Pass the Parcel', page 54 or 'Parcel Race', on page 84, would all make good topical games at a time when parcels are so much in the air, especially if Christmas wrappings were used; children could be asked to model a Father Christmas or a Christmas Tree out of plasticine; etc., etc.

A NEWSPAPER PARTY

Older children would get considerable fun out of a 'Newspaper Party'. Send out the invitations on a piece of folded board, covered with newspaper on the outside, and with the invitation written inside in the form of a news item.

Make hats, tablecloths, and other decorations out of newspapers. The tablecloths can be made quite attractive in the manner described on page 23 under 'Paper Doily'.

Some suitable games would be 'Hat Parade' and 'Make an Elephant', on pp. 43/4, 'Family Album', on page 46, 'Advertisements' (the second suggestion), on page 47, 'Untie a Parcel', on page 52, 'Pass the Parcel', on page 54, or 'Parcel Race', on page 84 (in each case wrapping the parcel in sheets of newspaper instead of brown paper); 'Newspaper Race' on page 86, 'Poisoned Carpet', on page 58, calling it 'Poisoned Newspapers', and using sheets of newspaper instead of a carpet; 'Chocolate Race', on page 34, putting a newspaper tablecloth over the bridge table; 'Hokey-Pokey', on page 30, and 'Paper Doily', on page 23 (older children will enjoy this as much as younger ones); etc., etc.

NURSERY RHYME PARTY

Another theme that is easily adapted and very appealing is that of Nursery Rhymes. Design for a motif some well-known Nursery Rhyme figure, easily recognized in outline, such as Miss Muffet's spider, Mary's lamb or Humpty-Dumpty. Alternatively, collect a number of small pictures of Nursery Rhyme characters from children's cheap picture books, and paste these on invitations, hats, sweet-baskets, name-places, etc. Try to introduce the Nursery Rhyme characters into table and food decorations in the same way – Humpty-Dumpty cakes, small mice made out of prunes with liquorice tails, biscuits in the shape of cats, mice, lambs, etc.

A novel centre-piece for the table would be a large pie-dish, topped with a pie-crust made from crepe paper representing the pie in which 'four and twenty blackbirds' were baked. Coming out from under the paper pie-crust have a number of strings, one for each child, either with their names on them or leading to their places. On the end of each string, under the pie-crust, would be tied a present for each child, which he or she would pull out in turn.

Ideas for games that could be played are 'Tommy Tucker', on page 27; 'Find Your Pair', on page 25, called 'Jack and Jill'; 'Cat and Mouse', on page 28 called 'Little Miss Muffet', the player outside the circle being a spider trying to get inside and catch Miss Muffet; 'Make an Elephant', on page 44, asking the children to tear out any well-known Nursery Rhyme character; 'Shoe Scramble', on page 26, called 'The Old Woman's Shoes'; 'Rob the Shop', on page 22, called 'Mother Hubbard's Cupboard', which would soon be bare; 'Feeding-Time', on page 39, using animals that feature in Nursery Rhymes and calling the different teams 'Tom's Pig', 'Mary's Lamb', 'Goosey-Goosey Gander', 'The Cat with the Fiddle', 'The Cow that Jumped Over the Moon', etc.; 'Spinning the Platter', on page 40, calling it 'The Dish that Ran Away with the Spoon'; 'Playing Trains', on page 25, calling it 'Ride-a-Cock Horse', one player in each pair being the rider, the other the horses, etc., etc.

A FAIRY-TALE PARTY

Similar to the Nursery Rhyme party above would be a 'Fairy Tale' party, with motifs and themes based on characters or objects taken from well-known fairy stories – Cinderella's pumpkin, a glass slipper, Red Riding Hood's cloak or basket, Puss-in-Boots' boots, etc.

Games and decorations could be adapted to fit Fairy Tale characters and themes in the same way as suggested for Nursery Rhymes.

AN ANIMAL PARTY

One of the easiest themes to develop would be one based on animals, which are always loved by children, and would therefore be very popular with them. There is a great variety of popular animals from which to choose for the main motif, having several different ones, and calling it a general 'Animal Party', or specializing on one particular animal and having a 'Dog Party', or a 'Cat Party', or a 'Horse Party'. These last suggestions would be very suitable if either the host or hostess or most of the guests were known to be especially interested in some particular animal.

You could either design a motif or have small pictures for decoration, as this is another instance where it would not be difficult to collect a large number of pictures of animals from cheap children's books, magazines, etc. Food decoration should also be easy, as one constantly sees recipes for children's cakes or biscuits in the shape of animals. Also, there are many cake-shops which specialize in making these.

The entertainment too, would be simply planned, as in preceding pages are a number of games that could be played without any alteration – 'Pinning the Tail on the Donkey', on page 19, 'Fishing Pond', on page 19 'At the Zoo', on page 21, 'Modelling', on page 22, 'What Am I Like?' on page 24, 'Cat and Mouse' and 'What's the Time Mr. Wolf?' on page 29, 'Pussy Wants a Home', on page 31, 'Fox and Geese', on page 32, 'Feeding Time', page 39, 'Make an Elephant', page 44, 'Name It', page 50, 'Apt Descriptions', page 64, 'Earth, Water Air', on page 74, etc., etc.

A SCHOOL COLOUR PARTY

Another very easy theme party to organize is one based on school colours, where all guests coming are from the same school. Use paper and board of the relevant colours for hats, baskets, decorations, etc. Buy balloons in the same colours. For invitations and place cards, very effective results can be obtained quite easily by merely drawing lines of the correct colours, with coloured pencils or water-colours, across the corners of pieces of white board.

Games, of course, could not be adapted to fit a colour scheme, but any prizes or parcels in 'parcel' games, such as described on pages 54, 55 and 58, could be wrapped in the correctly coloured papers.

FANCY DRESS PARTIES

If it were desired to have a Fancy Dress party, any of the themes discussed in this chapter would be very suitable and most popular. Children could be asked to come dressed as Dolls, Fairies, Nursery Rhyme characters, Cowboys, Indians, Fairy Tale characters, or any other subject you preferred.

The hostess should, however, think carefully before deciding on a Fancy Dress party. The children, of course, would love it, but one must remember that it would mean considerable work for the modern mother, already very hard pressed, and would also probably involve her in some extra expense. I think, therefore, that such a party should only be held on a very special occasion.

It may, however, be very suitable where a large charity, school or public party is being planned for some particular reason. Where several people are working for it, and where it is known that everyone is prepared to make a special effort to make the affair a success, a Fancy Dress party, based on one of the themes suggested in this chapter, with all the other aspects of the party carried out to fit in with the theme, could be a great success.

CONCLUSION

Many of the parties described in this chapter have had to be discussed much more briefly than originally planned. In addition, I had intended to suggest also a 'Circus Party', with animals, clowns, a merry-go-round, etc., as motifs; and an 'Historical Party', featuring famous people; also a 'School Party', using sheets from exercise books, coloured lead pencils, chalks, blackboards, etc., for invitations, decoration and games; and a 'Baby' party, with dummies and bottles to the fore. But, alas, our space has run out! I feel sure, however, that the ingenious hostess will have no trouble in following up the very brief suggestions we have been able to give, and will also be able to add, devise, and contribute many more ideas, both original and amusing.

Index

References printed in italics are the actual names of party games mentioned.

Party Games
And Ideas

by

Joyce Nicholson

Party Games And Ideas is packed with fun ideas for *adults'* party games. Joyce Nicholson outlines hundreds of ways to make a really successful evening.

She describes how to plan a party, break the ice, pair and mix guests and organise competitions. She also gives treasure hunt ideas, suggests having evenings of team competitions and explains how to arrange quizzes and engagement parties.

This book is a treasurehouse of ideas, games and themes which are guaranteed to make any party a memorable one.

How To Run
A Quiz

by

Dave Cornish

In this book Dave Cornish explains all things that need consideration when organising and running a quiz.

An experienced hand at quizzes – on both sides of the question table – he is able to show what makes a good format for a quiz evening and what makes a good set of questions.

However, not only does he explain how to set questions, he also gives over 2,000 example questions for immediate use. When you realise just how many are needed for a successful evening you'll be delighted with them and especially with the fact that they are grouped in order of difficulty under subject headings for easy reference.

In short, this book contains everything you need for planning a successful quiz evening!

In our Paperfronts *series*
(Standard paperback size)

Magic MAGIC
For All The Family

by

Geoffrey Lamb
(an associate of the Inner Magic Circle)

This book is just what you need to keep childen happily entertained at parties or for amusing family and friends after dinner.

It will enable *anyone* to become an 'apprentice magician'! There are over 60 tricks/puzzles – from delightfully easy match tricks to more intriguing and elaborate card tricks. No complicated hand movements are required or special props (just everyday objects) and the tricks don't need hours of practice! Hints on the all important art of performing are also given.

Master fascinating tricks like *Psychic Jack* and *Money Makes Money*. Make a lady vanish! Prove you have water divining powers, a magnetic finger and a detective's skill at picking out criminals!

In our Paperfronts *series*
(Standard paperback size)

Teach Your Child To Read Properly!

by

Niels Madsen

This book is for parents who are dissatisfied with the progress their child is making with reading at school. It is also for those who want to know how to start teaching their pre-school child to read.

Share Niels Madsen's 20 years' experience of teaching reading to young children (both as a class teacher and as a headmaster). He knows exactly how children really do *learn quickly*.

Reading is simply a matter of combining the "sounds" of individual letters. The child *must* recognise which letters represent which "sounds" and then be able to join the "sounds" together.

No parent who sees this book need fear that their child's reading will fall behind. They can do something about it, sure in the knowledge they are using proven principles.

RIGHT WAY
PUBLISHING POLICY

HOW WE SELECT TITLES

RIGHT WAY consider carefully every deserving manuscript. Where an author is an authority on his subject but an inexperienced writer, we provide first-class editorial help. The standards we set make sure that every **RIGHT WAY** book is practical, easy to understand, concise, informative and delightful to read. Our specialist artists are skilled at creating simple illustrations which augment the text wherever necessary.

CONSISTENT QUALITY

At every reprint our books are updated where appropriate, giving our authors the opportunity to include new information.

FAST DELIVERY

We sell **RIGHT WAY** books to the best bookshops throughout the world. It may be that your bookseller has run out of stock of a particular title. If so, he can order more from us at any time—we have a fine reputation for "same day" despatch, and we supply any order, however small (even a single copy), to any bookseller who has an account with us. We prefer you to buy from your bookseller, as this reminds him of the strong underlying public demand for **RIGHT WAY** books. Readers who live in remote places, or who are housebound, or whose local bookseller is unco-operative, can order direct from us by post.

FREE

If you would like an up-to-date list of all **RIGHT WAY** titles currently available, please send a stamped self-addressed envelope to

ELLIOT RIGHT WAY BOOKS,
KINGSWOOD, SURREY, KT20 6TD, U.K.